The Tales Of The Tails

Every Rescue Dog Has a Story

Steve Kravetz

Copyright ©2021 Steve Kravetz

No part of this work may be reproduced, stored in retrieval System or transmitted in any form, or by any means, electronic, Mechanical, photocopying, recording, or otherwise without Prior permission in writing from the author or publisher.

ISBN: 9-780-999635575

Published by Steve Kravetz

Cover design by: jbinspiration@fiverr

Dedication

This book is dedicated to my wife of twenty eight years Darlene Harris Kravetz, who passed over the Rainbow Bridge in 2016. I am sure she was greeted by many of her four legged tail-wagger.

Fortunately I met another woman a few years ago who loved all dogs as much as I do, my wife Louise, a retired dog walker and mother to Victoria and Vivian, both rescues.

The last dedication is to the thousands of people who have been in the past or are currently active in Dog Rescue.

THANK YOU ALL

Table of Contents:

It is all in the Name..1
In the Beginning...2
The Cause...3
A Chicken for a dog: Pug...5
Christian..7
Momma: Rita..10
New Beginning/ New Lady and New Dog: Wally...................13
The Trouble Maker: Toby...16
Dog Rescue Becomes Part of Our Life....................................19
The $22,000 Dog: Nick...32
The Sergeant-at-Arms: Sake...34
The Psycho Dog: Mookie...37
The Herd, Six Wild Maltese...39
The Bear: Yogi..41
Marty the Mouth..43
Tri-ped: Luke...45
The Terror: Ty..47

Surprise Find: Little: Miss Tinkles..49
Sweet Teddy...51
Bright Eyes: Billy..52
Ryan aka: Mad Max...54
Rescues who made it to the, "Big Time and Fame".................57
News Paper Reporters: Harry Gareth Edward Spaulding Puli-at-Large and the Fisch..59
Author: Steve Kravetz...61
Happy Endings...63

The Rescues Who Made It to, "The Big Time."

Rin- Tin -Tin 57
From Old Yellow: Spike...57
TV and Movie Star: Benji..58
From Annie: Sandy..58
From TV's, Full House: Buddy 58
Authors: Harry & the Fitch from coloryourstory.com............60

It is all in the Name

The good Lord created all the animals in our world and, they numbered in the thousands. He gave the task of naming them all to Adam, except one. This one animal had a special place in his heart. God gave him his own name… GOD aka DOG.

In the Beginning

In the beginning canines and humans had a love-hate relationship. Both were hunters, thus competitors and often after the same prey, but somewhere in time they joined forces one on one. Man found a loyal companion, and work mate. The canine found they needed and enjoyed human contact and approval. Ever since the two have been inseparable, each being better because of the other.

The Cause

Rescuing abused, neglected, and lost canine souls, and finding them a home with new families who will love them no matter what their past has been, takes a special person. Dog rescues are made up of lots of these wonderful loving people. They for the most part are volunteers, whose time is spent making sure the animals have been groomed and their health issues both physical and mental have been addressed. They often time keep the animal in their own home until a new forever home can be found. These people get much more love and satisfaction back for all the time, money, and effort they put out. One of the biggest rewards comes from seeing a dog and their new owner first meet and fall in love.

For over a decade my wife, Darlene Kravetz, and I were involved with Non-Profit Dog Rescues. First as volunteers, taking dogs into our home, until the right forever home was found. We transported animals when needed to the vets, to events, and to meetings with potential adoptees.

Then as proprietors of our own rescue, "For the Love of a Lhasa" a 501 c/non-profit rescue, which operated for over eight years.

During these years many dogs came across our door. Each dog had a story, and from that long list we have a few stories I wish to share. So sit back and enjoy some great heart felt stories/tales of tails of wonderful dogs.

Profits from the sale of this book will be shared by several rescues.
If you have a special animal rescue you would like to be considered for donation funding, please leave a message on authorstevekravetz.com

A Chicken for a dog: Pug

My love for animals started late one afternoon while I was at the State Fair of Texas in Dallas. I was six years old, and my family was enjoying the sights, sounds, food, rides, and, of course games of chance, opportunities to win a stuffed animal.

I was flipping nickels on the Midway and as luck would have it I put one on the plate without it falling off. My reward was not a big stuffed bear but a live baby chicken, aka Miss Peep.

My dad built a box for her and added sawdust for the floor. It was my job to feed and change water and the poopy sawdust. Each week she grew as did the smell, but I loved her and dutifully took my job seriously.All went well until very early one morning Miss Peep started crowing. She was a he and his natural behavior was causing problems. My father, being a practical man swapped

Mr. Peep for a Boston Bull Terrier that was a year old. Pug, as she was to be known, was an important part of our family. She taught me responsibility of taking care of something besides myself. She was a play mate for my brother, and always ready to participate in any of our family's activities.

No matter how long I had been gone, like when I went off to college or just out to the mail box, she was always glad to see me and was front in center. She was to be the official tail-wagging greeter to all of those who crossed our threshold.

She was my first dog but by no means my last. I was always to have a dog of my own in my life, except the four years I went off to college.

Christian

Following graduation, I moved into the second floor of an old duplex in Dallas. After about six months there, I decided I needed a dog, so I went to the City of Dallas's pound one rainy Sunday afternoon just after Christmas. I lucked out because a breeder had just dropped off three Golden Retriever six month old dogs. She could no longer sell them as puppies, and the prime buying season had passed, these were her left overs. Two were beautiful females, but the male was the one that grabbed my attention. My girlfriend of the time and I could not stop laughing at his antics, so Christian as he was to be known came home with us. We set up a routine and he was housebroken in just a few days.

The first several weeks went well. He loved chasing the ball, and when on walks always brought attention from the neighborhood kids, who loved to play ball in a vacant lot behind our home. About six weeks after he came home with us, my lady came home from work with a full bladder, as was Christian's too. She let him out back to the yard, which had no fencing, to do his business, while she went in to do hers. When done, she came out to find him gone. It was a Friday night, and when I got home, we both looked high and low, calling his name, still no luck. I had work the next day but she with the help of the kids from the neighborhood searched all over again, but still no luck. Sunday rolled around and we began visiting area pounds to see if he had been picked up while he was loose. Still no luck, but when we got home late that afternoon, there by the back door was my dog, waiting patiently. Around his neck was what was left of a rope. Where he had been and who took him we never found out, but I knew for sure that he knew where he belonged, and who his people were.

He loved to travel. No matter if he was in the snow, because I went skiing, or at the beach, he made the best of it, rolling in the snow, or digging in the sand chasing sand crabs.

I had a wonderful lady and after we were married life, we bought our first house. One Saturday my wife Julie decided to have a garage sale and advertised. I helped set it up before I went off to work.

The sale went well. Christian was there the whole time keeping her company as he often did. Just before she was about to close a man got very aggressive with his negotiations, getting quite loud. He made a fast movement toward Julie, and before he made his second step forward, he found all 120 pounds of dog facing him, then Christian jumped up on his hind legs, and had one paw on each side of the man's shoulders. Face to face with the dog now growling, showing his teeth and pushing the man back. The intruder left quickly and the dog went back to his place under the table.

He lived to be 14 years old and gave us many great years of joy.

His end also was about the time my marriage ended too.

Momma: Rita

I worked with a guy who had found a young Golden Retriever female and after putting out notices, and not getting any hits he kept her. Rita became her name and she must have been about two years old. Jerry worked two jobs, leaving early in the morning and not coming home until late at night. Rita, when bored, could be mischievous. So, Jerry started to leave her out during the day. She soon found she could jump or climb over the four foot fence. She loved to travel the area, and Jerry found he was getting calls at work, Rita was here or there. Thank goodness she had her tags.

After months of her running away, I suggested he find her another home where she could get more attention. My best friend, Harry was looking for a dog and so Rita now had a new home and owner. Rita turned out to be a great dog, and as Harry moved from place to place and city to city she easily adapted. Harry moved down to Freeport, Texas to run a fuel business on the intra-coastal canal. Rita would be the first one to greet the tugboats that came in to refuel, as well as large pleasure boats that the business serviced. In late afternoon she would go for a swim to cool off before dinner. One day Rita went into the water later than normal and the tide was going out. It took her out without Harry noticing. Later that night he got a call from the gate keep at one of the Dow Chemical Company's plants. She asked if he was missing his dog, she saw one that looked like Rita being pushed into the large complex. It would take Harry and a security Guard four hours to find her. She had found her way out of the water, and was lying in a doorway. She was nearly bald, the chemicals having eaten her hair and she was sick for a few days.

Another time a Tug had come into dock late one afternoon just before sunset. Harry went out to help the captain tie off the barge he was pushing before he could pull up to be fueled. Harry as walking across the field when Rita came up behind him, she jumped on his back knocking all six foot of Harry, down. Rita then jumped over Harry quickly.

She only took a couple of steps then yelped and dropped. What Harry found was that she had been bitten by a rattlesnake. She was rushed to the vet and though sick and swollen but still alive. She heard the snake and saved Harry's life.

Years later Harry relocated to Midland, Texas and moved into a typical housing development, which had lots of kids. Rita always drew kids to her. Every afternoon the area kids would knock on Harry's door asking if Rita could come out and play. Her skill with balls was second to none. If though, the ball would go into the street, she would not let any of the kids into the street to retrieve it. She would use her nose to guide the child back to the sidewalk, then go get it herself.

She and Christian had one litter of puppies. I saw an ad one morning in the newspaper, "Looking for female farm dog with a litter of pups for area movie shoot." One look at our group and it was a done deal, Rita and her puppies would become movie stars in an area shot of, "Of Mice and Men." a local production that Robert Blake was staring in, an also directing and producing. I was to become the puppy wrangler on that shoot.

New Beginning/ New Lady and New Dog: Wally

As happens when one major event in our life hap-pens it becomes a catalyst for other actions. I found myself without a dog and wife at the same time, until I met Darlene, the woman who would share my life and love for dogs for the next twenty eight years.

We both grew up with dogs playing a big part in our lives. We had been together for six months when we were out shopping. We came upon a rescue in the mall. They had several dogs, but one kept coming up to Darlene. We were to find out this dog had been placed in not one but two different homes but had been returned. The rescue lady told us he had been removed from a puppy mill and they thought he was a Shih Tzu mix of some kind. He was shaved down, and was a beautiful golden color, and he had the most amazing dark teary eyes. Wally, as he was to be called turned out to be a great dog. Smart easy to train. As he matured and his hair grew out what we found was a beautiful Lhasa-Apso. We never knew what the cause was for his returns from his previous owners, but their loss was our luck.

In the years to come he would be the lead dog of the pack, no matter if the dog was staying temporary or staying forever. He was a very Zen dog. On family vacations to the beach he liked walking in the sand but no interest in the water. He preferred to climb into the empty lifeguard chairs and just stare out to the horizon watching wave after wave come in, sometimes for hours at a time.

He loved to be dressed up and once when partici-pating in a fourth of July dog show he was dressed in his red, white, and blue's and walked around the ring with Darlene leading him. Head high and tail wagging, prancing proudly Wally knew he looked good. When he got to the judges table he slowed down, looked up, and with confidence, he put two front paws on the table. Then took a moment and gave all the judges a big smile before barking once. Wally then jumped down and continued walking around the track.

He did not win first place, but got dog with the big-gest personality award.

When we first got Wally we were living in an apartment. On Wally's first birthday Darlene threw him a birthday party. She invited all the kids in the com-plex to the party. We had several other dogs join the festivities along with about eight kids. She served cupcakes to the kids and some summer animal treats for the dogs. She had hats for everyone and even a few games with prizes. All the kids left with gift bags. This was not his only party but certainly the most famous.

Wally lived to be fourteen before his kidneys gave out. He would be the motivation for Darlene's "For the Love of a Lhasa," 501-c non-profit dog rescue.

The Trouble Maker: Toby

In her senior year of college, Shelly, Darlene's old-est child, was too adopted from the Denton City pound Toby. A Poodle -Bichon mix, that was about eight months older than Wally, and they were very close. We had at the time a cat named Muncie. Toby loved to terrorize the cat every opportunity he got. Toby came to stay after Shelly moved off to grad-uate school, and poor Muncie's life got worse. She figured out how to get her revenge. Though she was declawed, she would lie in wait on an ottoman and as Wally and Toby chased each other around it, she would pound Toby on the top of his head every time he came back around. Driving him crazy and not knowing where it was coming from.

On our trips to the beach, where Wally hated the water Toby loved it. The beach meant freedom. On our first trip to the beach, after walking miles with

Toby being crazy. He loved chasing crabs, and jumping in and out of the water. Wally ventured near the water's edge, stuck his head down to smell the water. He had all four of the bottom of his feet submerged about an inch, when the tail end of the next wave splashed him in the face. He had such a look on his face, but before he shook his head and walked out of the surf. Wally looking back once, as if to say, "This is what you are so excited by, why?"

We lived on a large lake and after several dry winters the lake was down and quite muddy for several hundred feet before you got to the water line. Toby and Wally had spent the day at the groomers, and Darlene had them back home and out back to walk them. At the shore line was a flock of Mallard ducks. One look at them and Toby was off. He hit the end of his leash, pulled his head out from his collar and the race was on. Now ducks are smarter than they look especially when being chased by a determined dog. When Toby hit the muddy shoreline he just slid first. He joyfully galloped through it. When hitting water's edge he doubled down and swam after a group of three. Each time he would get closer they would just fly further out into deeper and deeper water. My concern now was if he continued he might get tired out in the middle of the lake, then be too tired to swim back. Darlene ran back to the house and got his favorite toy and dog treats, waving them in the air and yelling for him to come and get it. Fortunately, he turned around and did head back to the shore and his treats. I ended up having to rewash and dry him before he could come back inside the house. Toby was a funny dog, loved toys, especially one rubberized squeaky that he would squeak and squeak then toss it across the room, and promptly run after, starting the solo game all over again.

He was the oldest in the group when he moved in with us, and been the number one dog when he was living with Shelly, still when he did come to stay, he never challenged Wally for dominance of our growing pack.

Dog Rescue Becomes Part of Our Life

By this time Darlene had been actively involved in dog rescue for a couple of years working with a Houston based group. We would have dogs, who came and went fast and others that never left. With burning desire to do more, Darlene decided to open her own **501-C** non-profit dog rescue. It was to be called, "For the Love of a Lhasa." {FTLOAL} The next eight years she ran it full time eventually having a branch in Rockwall/ Dallas and a second office outside Houston. The organization would have at least eight people who would foster [making sure the dogs were cared for, had been seen by vets, groomed, and even behavioral trainers] at their homes. Most of the time the foster family paid out of their own pockets for food and grooming, Doctors and medical bills FTLOAL would cover. The FTLOAL Rescue was placing between the two branches 35 to 45 dogs a year. That required lots of phone and face to face work besides all the paper work and paying bills. Raising funds from people who cared, in itself was a full time job. The vet bills were always in need of funds to cover all the issues some of the dogs had, and which were addressed before they were to be put up for adoption.

Likewise, each family who wanted to adopt one of our dogs went through a vetting process. Refer-ences were checked and communication with their veterinarian followed through. If at all possible a home visit was set up with the dog, so backyards and fences could be checked and to see how the dog and family interacted with each other, with kids and other pets if the home had them.

Weekends were for that travel, so to meet with candidates, for Darlene would not just give anyone of her babies. Each potential adoptive family went through an investigation. If possible, an in- person meeting with the dog to make sure it would be a great fit. We also would meet up in Centerville with Diann who was running the Houston branch of FTLOAL to exchange dogs. This was done at least once or twice a month. Dog shows were a great way to advertise and get show goers to open their pock-ets and maybe find an interest in one of our dogs looking for a forever home, and were events we participated in, when possible.

To have a successful business you must run it as a business, so too with a 501-C, the state and federal governments wanted paper work. If you are out of funds you close or in this case, reach into our own pockets to cover any month's shortages. It was certainly a very, non-profit for us, but our rewards were many.

We received dogs from City pounds, County's various animal control programs or SPCA raids on puppy mills, or breeders who had neglected their animals. Often after one of these raids there might be dozens of different type breeds and fifty or more dogs. Established rescues would be contacted, if they had maybe 4 dogs that were Lhasa or Shih-Tzu, or small breed we might get a call, "can you take these four dogs." The pit bull rescue would be called for their type of dogs, ect. We would go to dog auctions for breeders. We would try to buy as many dogs as possible, to get them away from a life as a breeder. Darlene over the years made connections with other rescues throughout the country and they often worked together.

One of her connections was a volunteer, who lived in West Texas, and whose family's business was in oil field supply. She often ran a truck and trailer up to puppy mill area's and made her known to local vets who worked these area's puppy mills. She relayed the message, "that if they had a pup that was brought in by a breeder to be put down because they did not meet the breeds standards. Say one ear goes up the other one goes down. If the dog was still healthy she would pick the dogs up when she was back in the area in a week or so."

Dogs come from all different backgrounds as you shall see with the next dogs.

Toby beating up on his arch-enemy Muncy the cat.

Young buddies hanging out on the bed, Toby and Wally

Wally's first birthday party

Marty n Yogi at home.

Wally getting into the Christmas spirit.

Traveling Tilly

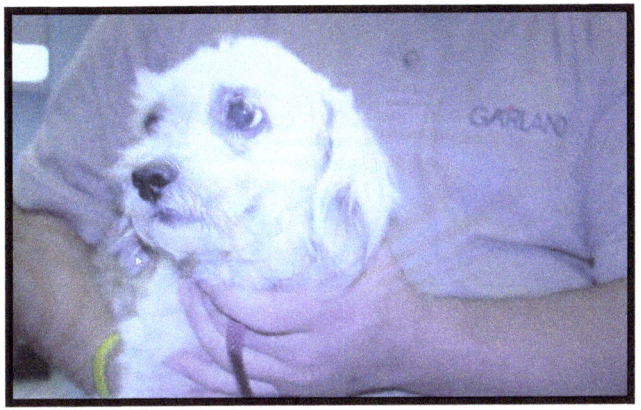

Rescue dog being picked up from the local pound

Participants at a local adoption event

Rescue Dog waiting for new adopters to take him to his new forever home

Our pack at the beach

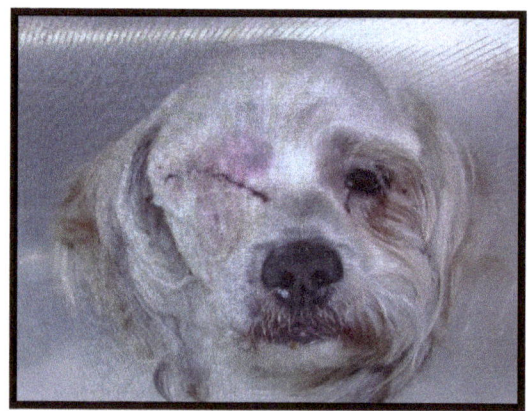

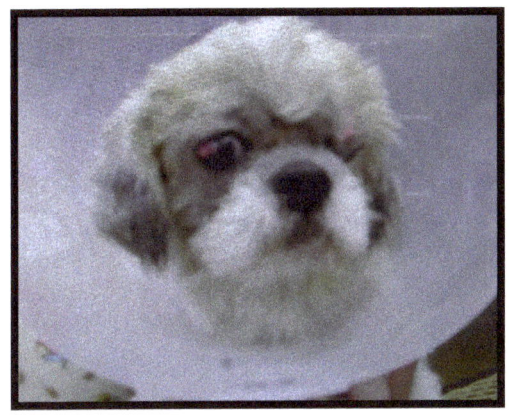

first pictures after visiting the Veterinarian for need repairs

Just a few more happy rescued dogs

The $22,000 Dog: Nick

It was a late-night call from a member of Fort Worth's SPCA one Saturday that would bring Nick to our attention. The raid on a puppy mill just outside of town that day brought them twenty dogs and Nick had been one of the ones who needed a lot of care. He seemed to be about three. His coat had been shaved. His eyes were a mess, infected and swollen shut. We found out he had been a breeder, and when not breeding was stuck in a cage with two other cages above him. The other dogs' urine had dripped down on him and infected his eyes. We would also find out he had never walked on grass. Despite all his problems he was such a gentle soul and would grow out a soft black and silver-grey coat. Nick became the alpha dog of the pack and everyone's favorite, over the years though Nick had many health

problems. He had two surgeries just on his spine, and one for kidney stones removal. Two of the surgeries were done at Texas A&M College of
Then one at Oklahoma States University Veterinary College. Both universities gave the rescue a break in the surgery cost. Still in all over the years we spent $22000.00 on Nick's health care. His quite manor seemed to extend to all the other dogs. When we traveled on trips he was the first out of the car, first to check everything out. When we went to the beach he loved to walk on the sand, but like Wally he too had no interest in getting wet or playing in the waves. He though did love watching the water roll in, like his predecessor.

The Sergeant-at-Arms: Sake

Sake was a full-blood Lhasa, white all over except for a brown spot on his rump. He had the longest canine teeth: over an inch longer than any Lhasa I would ever meet. He came to us from the Houston pound. The animal control officers had tried to catch him for two weeks. He kept running away when he saw them. When he was finally caught he had a piece of rope around his neck, no collar. He was matted to the skin and his nails were so long they cured back onto his pads. Mostly he was an angry biting dog. The Houston pound was glad to get rid of him and not have to put him down.

By the time he came into our rescue he had been shaved, nails done and given good food. He was still a mad biting dog, so because I had had some success with these type dogs he was traded off to us from Houston, for me to work with him. His first couple of days he just fitting in to the small pack we had at the time. The third day as I walked past him as he was eating, he nipped me. I turned around, grabbed him by the scuff of the neck, lift-ed him up off the ground and shook him hard. Saying,"No,No,No," then putting him back on the ground. He shook his head, looked up at me with the, 'What the hell,' look, then went back to eating. About a week later was another incident with him nipping at me. I again picked him by his neck and shook him then put him down. He looked up and had the most confusing look on his face. This picking up and shaking is behavior a mother dog does to her pups to bring them in line. Then on a rainy day, I put him on leashes to take out. When he got to the door he stopped and sat down. I would find out then, that Sake did not like the rain. I picked him up took him out and used an umbrella over him. He got to business fast, and I could tell he was so glad he did not get rained on. That act of kindness seemed to change his attitude.

Sake loved working the dog shows, were we had a booth. He would trot into the crowd that walked in front of our table. Smile and leads people back to our booth. At one Houston show our booth was next to the Mastiff rescue. Sake went up to one of the big dogs, and when the bigger dog bent his head down to sniff Sake. My boy just licked the bigger dogs face, and smiled, as only

Sake could, and for the next two days the two hung out when not working the show.

Sake was one of those dogs who loved toys, especially ones that squeaked or talked like the cow that mooed, or pig that squealed. One holiday Darlene bought him a Tickle me Elmo doll. He was in love, and played with it for hours and hours. Then the next year she bought him Care Bears. They were even a bigger hit. In the middle of the night we would hear. "I love you!" or "You're my best friend!" Thankfully none said, "Let's go outside and play now." He loved that they talked to him.

Sake took to Nick from the very start. He sensed Nick's weaknesses and became his protector. With those big canines and his asserted style, Sake could be a dog to be reckoned with. Usually, it only took a serious growl or bearing of his teeth to back any-thing off. What he considered might be a threat to Nick. They just seem to have a special bond between them.

The Psycho Dog: Mookie

Mookie came to the Houston group because another rescue had taken him to a Vet to put down. He was a biter, big time. The dog's canines had been ground down and even had rubberized caps put on. He was just a psycho dog. He was part Poodle and part Lhasa. As I was about to find out was not a good cross. The vet called our group in Houston to see if we would take him. Because I had had success with Sake he was traded up to us. Mookie was certainly crazy in many ways. If you picked him up to love on him he would growl like he was going to kill you, but at the same time he loved it. If he was lying on the ground and you walked past him, again he would go crazy snarling, growling, and even snap-ping. If you stopped and turned around 360 degrees when you came back around and faced him, he was just fine. He of course snapped at me and I gave him the pick- up by the scuff of the neck, shake and put down treatment. Unlike Sake, this would only make him madder if possible. I tried it several times over the first few weeks he was with us. Despite all my attempts to correct Mookie's behavior, nothing worked. Just the same Mookie loved being a part of the pack, even if it was at the bottom. He thrived and when on vacation at the beach loved the sand and more, he loved digging. He would chase sand crabs, digging after them when one slipped into their holes. If he was not chasing crabs he would dig just to kick up sand and because he loved it. He would jump in the surf and up at the birds. A lot like Toby, the poodle in him, I guess. Over the years he mellowed some, Mookie also loved when Darlene would dress him up for Halloween. He would strut his stuff with his costume on, with a smile on his face. Over time he and I had a truce of sorts. I let him be his crazy self and he would growl a little less, a very little less.

The Herd, Six Wild Maltese:

Just when one crisis is handled at least one more or two would come in with a phone call from a vet or pound somewhere. This time the call was from a neighbor of a breeder in Oklahoma. His neighbors got a divorce and both left the property and just let the dogs go free, they were running loose through the neighborhood. The county government did not have interests in handling the problem. Somehow a neighbor got Darlene's rescues phone number. She drove up to the site by herself, and hired a few high school kids to help wrangle the pups. As it turned out of the ten dogs six were Maltese. They were the hardest to catch, quick, small, and could hide in small spaces. The other dogs Darlene was able to place while there. The neighbor who found one of the dogs, a cocker, fell in love. The three paid help swapped out pay for the three beagle pups that they found. So Darlene came home late that night with six Maltese, yappy pups.

The pups went through the usual, soap, n water, clip, clip, and then off to the vet we used. Many vet offices will discount bills for rescues, including surgery's needed for neutering or broken legs, eye removals, etc. plus the needed treatments, heart worm testing and treatment if needed. Then of course, their normal shots all dogs need. Vet bills are the largest expense each month for most rescues.

In the end they all found a new forever homes in less than three weeks, though they really livened up our house while they were around.

The Bear: Yogi

We bought Yogi from a breeder in our area. The lady would not allow us to come to her place but wanted to meet in a Walmart parking lot. When we did purchases like that or went to auctions of breeders, we would not reveal that we were rescuers. Yogi was a big Lhasa, and most like had some Tibetan Terrier in him as well. When we first got him his coat of black with just a touch of gray, felt like straw, probably from the cheap dog food he had been given. In the following months his coat softened up with an improved diet and added vitamins Darlene was feeding him. Yogi got his name because he would sit up on his two hind legs, front paws out and down. He looked just like one of those chain saw cut bears, cut out of a piece of tree trunks. Yogi, though the biggest size-wise of the pack was just a big teddy bear. He was pure joy. Always happy and never gave much thought to his position in the growing numbers of our pack. The dog was never sick, never had behavioral problems, love people and was gentle with kids. He too loved the beach, and could walk forever, never tiring. Thankfully, because Yogi weighted almost thirty eight pounds and was too heavy to carry very far.

He too liked to get dressed up and always had a natural smile on his face.

We had to go to a family event out of town and could not take the dogs, so we hired a friend to stay at the house and dog and house sit for a few days. We had been gone for just a day when Louise called our dog sitter Melisa to see how things were going with the guys.

Melisa related to Louise this story. She had put all the dogs to bed and had been asleep herself for several hours, when out of the darkness, she distinctly heard, "Hey you." she awoke up to hear it again, "Hey, you." She got out of bed, got a gun out of her bag slowly she went down stairs searching the whole house finding nothing. Again just as she was going back up-stairs she hear it clearly, she turned only to find Yogi. It had been Yogi hacking, which he would do from time to time and if you did not know, it did sound like, "Hey you."

Marty the Mouth

Marty was not supposed to come to us. He was a young white Maltese with a heart condition. Diann, the Houston counterpart to Darlene, had brought him with her to place with a couple on her way to Centerville to meet us after his placement. The couple decided to go with a different dog, and so Marty was there at our bi-monthly exchange. The minute Diann opened her car door, Marty was out took one look at Darlene and ran as fast as his little paws would go, and planted himself between Darlene's legs. It would be exactly where you would find him for the next dozen years. He did not want to be on our bed at night, instead on the floor so he could be there if she decided to get up and go anywhere.

Marty was a talker/barker. He had such an attitude in a very short time once in the pack. He was cute, spunky, but he had been born with a heart murmur, and in the end stopped two different families to adopt him. So he became a forever foster. He was shy in his own way, only letting Darlene pick him up without a chase. She had a way with animals, they knew her heart, and responded to her in kind. Mar-ty was a very sweet dog, despite his barking which drove me crazy. The last nine months of Darlene's life were hard. She was in the hospital twelve times. It was always the hardest on Marty. He would lay by the front door waiting patiently. On weekends sometimes I would take Marty with me when visiting the hospital. They both got such a kick out of the time.

It was Marty who alerted me to Darlene's passing. She was home in bed upstairs asleep after lunch and meds. About one that after noon, Marty ran down-stairs, sat in front of me, and began to bark at me, as to say, "Follow me," as he ran back upstairs. Darlene had passed over the Rainbow Bridge herself.

A week later, I found Marty too, had passed on over the Rainbow Bridge to follow his momma. He lived six years longer than anyone thought he would.

Tri-ped: Luke

Luke came to us via Vet from Dallas as a referral. Luke was part Lhasa, and part Tibetan terrier. He was a big puppy who had gotten a front leg infected somehow. Because the owner waited too long to get it looked at by a Vet, gangrene set in and his right front leg had to be removed. When the owner did not come back to pick him up, Darlene was given a call for help.

Luke was a beautiful white long-furred dog with streaks of tan, and almost looked like an expensive toy when he was lying still. He was to become a member of our tribe, at least for a short while.

Luke learned to walk, jump and get by on his three good legs with some training. He never let what he did not have stopped him for what he want-ed. A visit from our daughter Shelly and

Son–in-Law David, who lived in San Francisco, was to find him his forever home. One look by Shelly and she was in love with him and his can -do spirit. She and David worked hard to continue to strengthen his legs and prepare him for the new life of big city dog, now living with lots of climbing stairs and hilly streets. Even though it is very hard on a dogs frame to take the force on only one front leg instead of two he never complained. He was one of those rare dogs who were loved by everyone he met. "Often you would see his whole face lite up when he was walking on the street and ran into some he knew," Shelly often said.

One young man in Luke's neighborhood called him a "Spirt Animal" because of his steely resolve to carry forth despite his handicap.

He lived to be 13 years old and always put smiles on every ones faces he met.

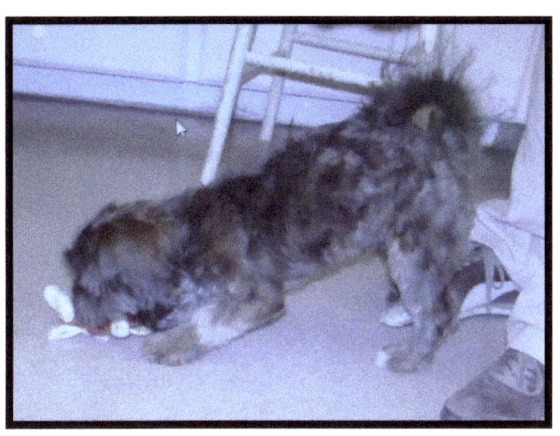

The Terror: Ty

Ty came to us from the Dallas pound. He had been turned in by his previous owners' boyfriend. It seemed when the boyfriend was around, the dog was put into an enclosed crate with only side holes and a small front grate. The boyfriend was jealous of Ty, so he would often kick the crate to mess with the poor dog. Finally, Ty became unmanageable when he was let out. Thus the boyfriend won that round. Ty was a beautiful Lhasa, brittle black and brown young dog not a year old. We also had no luck in taming him. So, after a month with no success Darlene looked for a trainer to help. What she found was Jay, whose back ground included growing up in Oklahoma on a Native American reservation with his grandparents. He had served in the military and now trained horses and security dogs. When Darlene first approached him he laughed in her face, "Lady, I train man eating animals." She just looked him in the Eye and said, "Great, I want you to turn this man eating animal back into a civilized dog. I f you can make them one way, you should be able to make them the other way. Jay took Ty and $2200 for the two months. In the end Darlene found a strong willed lady in East Texas who was looking for a dog like Ty, spunky. When Darlene went to pick him up, Jay was sad, he told her, that Ty had more heart in him than most of the big dogs he worked with and if he had room he would adopted himself. What he did do, is make a VCR tape for the new owner, to give her heads- up on Ty and what to expect and how to handle him. The funny thing Ty's new owner told Darlene years later was, if Ty got to acting up, all she had to do was put Jays tape in the VCR and no matter where Ty was, he would come running, sit in front of the TV and whine at Jay, and his behavior would change for the better.

Surprise Find: Little: Miss Tinkles

It was late November just before Thanksgiving, when Darlene got a call from our own vet. He had gotten a pup from one of his local clients who had found her last night, and did not want another animal at her place, "can we take her?" Miss Tinkles, as she was to be known for her short time with us came with a great story. The weather for this time of year was off, a cold front came through the day before and it was followed by rain, and light snow. The lady who found her was traveling home late from work. She lived deep in the country, off an old county farm road. The roads were slick and had ice forming and she was going slowly. Out of the corner of her eye she spotted something flopping around on the side of the road. She stopped, got out her flashlight and went to inspect. It was our girl. One of her ears was frozen to the road and she could not get herself free.

Our Good Samaritan got a tool out of her truck and was able to free the pup, she took her home for the night but took her to our mutual vet the morning of the call. She became a member of our pack, though she was so cute, and sweet, her stay with us was for less than a month. Her new forever home was to have two little girls who loved to dress her up and take her for wagon rides. We never found out how she got left out in the terrible weather, but in the end it was another happy- ending placement.

Sweet Teddy

Sweet Teddy came to us around sixteen weeks old. He was born to a champion Cocker Spaniel, who had a blind date with a Shih-Tzu.

We got a call from a small breeder who did not want to spend the money on fixing the dog's bad hernia that pushed his intestines out. A defect he had been born with.

Julia Moore took one look at him on our website and did not care if he had been born with a defect and was willing to wait until he had gone through the repair surgery before she could adopt him.

Darlene sent out an emergency E-Mail to her sup-porters for funds to help pay for Teddies needed operation.

Within a few weeks Teddy had his surgery and after-ward's Julia found she had a happy sweet, an affectionate dog. Over the years she would call Darlene every so often telling her of Teddy's latest escapade and how delightful she was to have him in her life.

Bright Eyes: Billy

Not all our dogs were puppies. Billy was one of the dogs which came to us by way of a call for help. His previous owner had to go to assisted living and could not bring his dog, Billy with him. He had been referred by a friend of FTLOAL. He appeared to be seven or eight years old but had been well cared for, and though not a pup anymore, his spirt was out going and he was adventurous. We always had a booth at area dog shows. It was at the 2008 Houston AKC dog show that Billy was to meet his new person. Dr. Seth Politano had been looking for a special dog for many months, but with no luck finding 'THE', dog. He was attending the dog show with his mom to watch the agility competition one of her favorite events, and not even thinking about his own search for the dog . Per the Drs. Words, "My life had changed and turned around in a few moments. Walking down an aisle, I saw Billy from afar, my mother and I could not help but to say hello to him. His eyes had a twinkle in them and when approaching him, he went on his back asking for a belly rub. Billy had me at that moment, the connection was immediate, and I knew by looking into his bright eyes the two of us were meant to be together."

The next five years the two went everywhere together. Houston to Southern California, to Arizona, and back to the beaches of California, Billy did not care even if he had to travel in a carrier under Seth's seat.

He loved treats but also loved to play tug of war with one of his favorites, the red bone, or stuff pink pig, and if they were not around his furry monkey would do.

The dogs always seem to know before anyone else, when that just right person was here for them.

Ryan aka: Mad Max

Not all dogs are a fit in their new home. Also not all people are prepared to deal with dogs that have behavioral problems. Ryan was one of those dogs. He had been placed in three different homes only to be returned three times. The rescue had him living the last five years with a volunteer. When I reached out to them to get his information they were ecstatic with my interest in him. My background in rescue and knowing I had worked with and had in the past troubled dogs seemed like a perfect fit.

The moment the dog came through our front door he ran past my wife and ran down the stairs. Took one look at me and laid down, rolled over on his back in front of my legs and smiled.

Ryan as he had been called was half Lhasa and half Poodle, and like Mookie he was a bit crazy. He was a leg lifter, no matter how much time he spent out-side or on walks he would mark his area. He had been neutered, but it did not stop him from marking. He also was a barker. I have never met a dog who loved to bark as this dog. Often times he would bark even if nothing was there just to hear his own voice. Lastly, he became fixated on guarding the front door. He bit a few of our guest's as they come in or go out. Come in the back door, he could care less.

His name was changed soon after he arrived, Max as he was to be called, because he looked like a Max more than Ryan. Soon fit in with our two other dogs and from the moment he came into our home he picked me to be his guy. If I let him, he would go anywhere I did, and he loved road trips anywhere. The beach though was paradise for him. He loved people, and often went up wagging his tail as we walked the beach meeting strangers..

Try as I might I could not break him of leg lifting, or barking, so we have worked out a quiet truce. I take him out more, less pee to deal with volume wise and I let him bark, but only for so long, we still have neighbors. He is one of the most affectionate dogs I have ever owned, and he loves to cuddle and be held. He is a regular sweetheart. Sometimes the most troubled dogs turn out to be the best ones, I also noticed every dog we had go through our door seemed to know when they reached their forever home. We could see it in their eyes and attitude.

Rescues who made it to the, "Big Time and Fame"

You will be surprised to know what famous dogs were rescues.

Radio, Movies and TV: Rin- Tin -Tin

Rinty was his name and Lee Duncan found him at a pound next to an old WW 1 battlefield. Lee took him home to America and the German Shepard, became an instant hit. His acting credits included silent movies, radio, and of course television.

Old Yeller's: Spike

Spike was a Yellow Mastiff/ Labrador Retriever, who was rescued by a friend of the famous Hollywood dog trainer Frank Weatherwax. He was found in the Van Nuys Animal Shelter near Los Angeles. The story goes he paid his friend three dollars for the dog.

TV and Movie Star: Benji

Frank Inn went into the Burbank Animal Shelter in 1960 on a hunch. What the animal trainer found was the 100 percent Mutt he had been looking for. This Cocker Spaniel/Schnauzer/Poodle mix was Franks' golden goose. Benji was to be seen on Beverly Hillbillies, Petty Coat Junction, Green Acres and The Walton's. Then on to the big screen in a list of his own Benji movies.

From Annie: Sandy

Sandy from Annie was hours away from being put down, when William Berloni came into the Connecticut Humane Society scouting for, "THE," dog the year was 1976. It was love at first-sight. The Beige Terrier mix was "THE" one he had been looking for. The show ran from 1977 through 1983 and the dog was the star every night. William paid a whopping eight dollars for the future Star Dog.

From Full House: Buddy

Buddy the beautiful Golden Retriever from the TV series Full House in season eight. Buddy was an-other member of the rescued club. Kevin Dicicco found him abandoned in the Mountains. Later Kev-in would say they rescued each other. This Star also too appeared in all Thirteen Air Bud motion pictures.

News Paper Reporters: Harry Gareth Edward Spaulding Puli-at-Large and the Fisch

Harry Gareth Edward Spaulding or HGES as he is known to his friends came all the way from Birmingham England. With the help of the PETCO Foundation who helped in locating Harry for Valerie Jagiello his new forever mom.

Valerie who is an artist, photographer, and writer used this personality-rich ham who loved to dress up as a model for some of Valerie creative work.

Yet HGES yearned to do more creative things and to expand his horizons. First Harry had to hone his own writing skills and when accomplishing that, he turned them in no time into a newspaper column, "Harry Gareth Edward Spaulding, Puli-at-Large."

As Harry started to write, he found himself beginning to interviewing all kinds of people for human interest stories. Some of their stories were about other animals rescued by area people and their successful adoptions. Some stories were about people who were rescued by dogs, and some stories were about the behind the-scenes workers who make res-cue work seem easy.

Local fame encouraged the two to move into children's books and expanding into the much in demand coloring book market. The newest addition to this working family is Allister the Fischer Edward Spaulding 111, a rescued Puli coming all the way from Oklahoma City. Soon the trios, who lived in New York City, were busy creating more art and coloring books.

A recent move to Texas the group now known as Valerie, Harry and the Fisch has expanded their de-sign custom conceptual coloring books. Check out @: www.coloryourstory.com

Author: Steve Kravetz

STEVE KRAVETZ was a born story teller, but not until 1994 did he ever write one down. It was this one, his first written tale that took home first place at the State Fair of Texas's Tall Tail/Lier's contest. This 74 plus year-old Rockwall Texas resident has published two successful literary fiction novels, but this non-fiction was a labor of love.

Happy Endings

Never does a day go by when I am sorry about the time we invested in this labor of love, or the tons of money we spent on these and the hundreds more we helped find their permanent home. I hope you enjoyed the tales of a few of them.

Remember only you can make the decision when looking for a new pet, to buy an AKC- type dog, or a dog in need of your love from a rescue.

www.ingramcontent.com/pod-product-compliance
Lightning Source LLC
Chambersburg PA
CBHW051553010526
44118CB00022B/2686